"Sappho Says..."

Poems and Fragments of Sappho of Lesbos

Translated by Frank Salvidio

Ibis Books
Falls Village, Connecticut 06031

"Sappho Says.."
Poems and Fragments of Sappho of Lesbos
Translated by Frank Salvidio
© 1999 Frank Salvidio

ISBN 0-935140-01-8

Published by Ibis Books
P.O. Box 133
Falls Village, CT 06031

For
the ankle-skirted teachers
of Broadway Grammar School (now no more)
in Norwich, Connecticut,
who—without preface or apology—
simply drilled the English language into my bones.

Contents

A Note on Reading the Poems

I have punctuated these translations to facilitate understanding, and not to indicate specific pauses. The commas and semi-colons are, for the most part, little more than "psychological tics," to be read right through, as though they were not there, particularly when the poems are read aloud, as they should be.

INTRODUCTION

Byron called her "burning Sappho," and borrowed from her, as Hardy did, and Housman. Catullus paraphrased her in passionate Latin verses addressed to the woman he called Lesbia, in her honor. Dante, who did not know Greek but did know Latin, sublimated Catullus' lines in the greatest sonnet of the *Vita Nuova*. Walter Savage Landor, who did know Greek, translated and expanded one of her fragments into a poem of his own. And Swinburne, who was obsessed with her, both celebrated and imitated her in his "Sapphics."

And they are not alone. For over 2,500 years, western poets—the great and the near-great, major and minor—have imitated and echoed Sappho of Lesbos, while empires and religions, nations and languages rose, flourished, fell and vanished. Among western poets, only Homer has lasted longer than Sappho—only Homer.

And yet, alas, this most celebrated (and probably greatest) of women poets exists for us today only in pieces—fragments, lines and phrases culled largely from the works of other, lesser writers, quoting her by way of example or illustration. Time and time again in the ancient texts we read the familiar words, or their equivalent: "Sappho says...."

And just who *was* this Sappho of Lesbos, this most famous and influential of women poets? The answer, unfortunately, is as fragmentary as her surviving poetry, and perhaps not even relevant. But if we need a living framework for her poetry, we may take as the agreed-upon "facts" of her life that she was born around 620 BC on the island of Lesbos; that she was married to a rich merchant from Andros, by whom she had a single child, a daughter named Cleis, after her own mother; that she had two or three brothers, one of whom was scandalously attached to an Egyptian courtesan, much to Sappho's displeasure; that she was famous during her lifetime, and that after her death she came to be regarded by the Greeks as their greatest lyricist.

And then, of course, there is her "reputation." Now, whether Sappho was the "head mistress" of some kind of finishing school for daughters of the well-to-do, the priestess of a cult devoted to the worship of Aphrodite, or one of a private group of girls and women bound together by intense emotional ties, the evidence—albeit wholly circumstantial—that she was a lesbian not only in name but in fact is overwhelming. And surely, it is principally because of her reputation as a "woman-lover" that to this day the word lesbian is more readily taken to mean a female homosexual than a native of Lesbos. It is no accident, after all, that the French word for lesbianism is *sapphisme,* or that Italians call lesbianism *amore saffico.*

In any case, suffice it to say that much of the extraordinary emotional intensity generated by her poetry owes its power to the fact that we take her words to be those of a woman in love speaking to, and about, other women; and that is the context in which I have made these translations.

As for the poetry itself, either God or genetics (or perhaps the Muse) gave Sappho an uncanny ability to make the language of ordinary speech fit her complex metrical patterns, as though the words could not have been arranged in any other way, and no other words could have been used. In reading the works of even the greatest of our own poets, we're often aware that the natural order of English speech has been compromised in accommodating rhyme and meter to achieve musicality. This is never the case with Sappho. And it is this ability to achieve music with natural expressions which is at the core of her art.

Unfortunately, it is not always possible to create music within the naturalness of ordinary speech in English, an uninflected language in which word order is crucial, as it is not in classical Greek. I have tried to resolve the problem of musicality by combining ordinary speech with occasional alliteration and an irregular iambic beat—iambic being the natural rhythm of English speech. In the "Hymn to Aphrodite," for example, I have used "Dapple-throned" instead of "many-colored" or "parti-colored," and "deathless" instead of "immortal," in order to produce the alliteration of

Dapple-throned, deathless Aphrodite,
Daughter of Zeus, wile-weaver:

And finally, although I probably would not have undertaken these translations if I had been completely satisfied with any of the existing ones, I have not made them to compete with the others. Rather, I urge anyone whose interest in Sappho is piqued by my translations to read the efforts of other translators. The reader may feel that I surpass in one poem and am surpassed in another; or that I both excel and am excelled in different lines of the same poem; or that I sometimes hit and sometimes miss the mark completely.

I shall not mind. After all, in the (Tenth) Muse's house there are many mansions—room enough, I trust, for all who serve her, and are of her train ("borrowed" from Milton, Sonnet I).

*Speak, now, holy lyre, make
your voice known through me.*

—Sappho

APHRODITE AND OTHER IMMORTALS

ॐ

Dappled-throned, deathless Aphrodite,
daughter of Zeus, wile-weaver: do not,
I beg you, mistress, break me with
hurt and grief;

but come to me here, instead,
if ever in time past you heard
my voice, far off, and left your
father's golden house,

drawn by your beautiful, swift sparrows
with whirring wings, down from heaven
through mid-air above dark earth,
to be suddenly here.

And then, blessed one, with a smile
on your immortal face, you asked me why
I had called you again, and what
my madding heart

most wanted now. "Whom must I persuade
this time into love? Who wrongs you,
Sappho?—for if she runs from you now,
she will follow;

if she won't take your gifts,
she will give them; and if she
does not love you, she will—soon
and unwillingly."

Come to me now again: deliver me from
hard anxiety; accomplish all that my heart
longs to see accomplished; and you yourself
be my fellow-fighter.

Hither to me from Crete, to this
holy temple in the delightful apple-tree grove,
where the altar is smoking with
incense;

where cold water murmurs through
the apple-tree boughs, and all the place
itself is shadowed by roses, and sleep
descends from shimmering leaves.

Here the meadow horses graze,
spring flowers blossom,
and the wind blows sweetly.

Here, Cypris, take and gently
pour in golden cups the nectar
mingled in our festivities.

Hesperus, bringing back all things
scattered in the shimmer of Dawn:
you bring the sheep, you bring the goat;
you bring the child to its mother.

Cypris, and you
Nereids, grant to my brother
that he arrive here unharmed;
and may all that he wishes come
completely to pass.

May he pay as well
for past failings, and be
in addition a joy to his friends,
poison to his enemies;
and to his sister be willing
to bring honor.

...the sister of golden-haired Phoebus, whom the daughter
of Coeus bore, having lain with the son of
Cronos, great of name:
but Artemis swore the gods a great oath:
"By your head, grant that I shall be an
unwedded virgin always, hunting beasts on the high
summits of the overlooking, lonely mountains. Come,
grant me this favor." Thus she spoke, and
the father of the blessed gods nodded indeed
his assent; and so men call her
the virgin huntress, shooter of deer—
a great commemoration; and Love, the limb-loosener,
never comes near her.

May she find you harsher, Cypris,
and so not boast—Doricha—saying
he came a second time to a longed-for love.

For it is not right
that there be lamentation
in the Muses' house.
That would not befit us.

"He is dying, Cytheria—
delicate Adonis!
What shall we do?"

"Batter your breasts, girls,
and tear your dresses."

Speak, now, holy lyre: make
your voice known through me.

Sweet mother,
I cannot work my loom:
delicate Aphrodite has
overcome me with love
for a boy.

"O master," I said,
"by the blessed one, I have
no pleasure above earth;
but long instead for the
underworld, and to see the dew
on the lotus banks of Acheron."

I spoke to you in a dream, Cyprus-born.

છે

Sing us the violet-robed one.

છે

Sweet-speaking Aphrodite

છે

    the violet-robed daughter of
the son of Cronos

છે

pain-giver

છે

tale-weaver

છે

you and my servant, Eros

Once again, Love, the limb loosener, shakes me—
an irresistible, bittersweet creature.

੨ഛ

Like a mountain wind
falling upon oak trees,
Love seized and shook my heart.

੨ഛ

They make me honored
with the gift of their works.

੨ഛ

If only I—O golden-throned Aphrodite—
could draw that lot.

Hither now, delicate Graces
and lovely-haired Muses.

ε🔊

Hither, holy Graces,
rosy-armed daughters of Zeus.

ε🔊

and you, yourself, Calliope

ε🔊

Leto and Niobe were dearest companions.

ε🔊

just as golden-sandalled Dawn

ε🔊

the gods give wealth

ε🔊

But the gods have no tears.

ε🔊

COMPANIONS

Equal of the gods he seems to me,
the man who sits opposite you,
listening to your sweet words
and lovely laughter,

which—truly—make my heart shake
in my breast; for if I see you
even for a moment, I cannot speak;
my tongue breaks,

and suddenly subtle fire burns
under my skin; my eyes
do not see; my ears hum, and sweat
pours from me;

I begin to tremble everywhere,
and, greener than grass,
I seem not far from death.

Truly I wish I were dead,
as she said to me often,

leaving with many tears:
"How illy we've been treated, Sappho,
and I go against my will."

And thus I answered her:
"Farewell, be happy,
and remember whom you leave shackled.

If you do not, I wish you yourself
to bear witness to how
lovingly we treated you:

for we wove garlands of violets
and roses and crocuses
for you, here beside me;

and twisted wreaths
around your neck; and you,
with perfume of flowers

befitting a queen, anointed yourself,
and here on soft pillows had
fulfillment of all you desired."

Some say a corps of cavalry, others of foot,
and still others that a fleet of ships
is the most beautiful thing on the dark
earth, but I say

whatever one loves is. This is readily
understood by all; for Helen—whose beauty
surpassed all mankind's—left the best of men
and sailed to Troy,

caring nothing for child or parents,
being lightly led by love. And now, although
she is not here, Anactoria is in my mind;
for I would rather

see her shining face, her lovely way
of walking, than all of Lydia's
chariots, or its armed and marching
infantry.

I bid you, Abanthis, take up
and sing of Gongyla, the lovely one,
while once again desire flies
around you, for even her dress,
when you saw it, excited you;
and I rejoice.

But if you are a friend to me,
win yourself a younger bed;
for I will not be the elder
in a companionship.

What country girl
enchants you now in
country clothes,
not knowing how to pull
her tattered dress
above her ankles?

    And you, O Dica,
put lovely garlands in your curls,
and bind dill together with your
delicate hands; for the blessed
Graces favor blooming flowers,
but turn away from the ungarlanded.

For when I look at you
opposite me, not even
Hermione is like you;
and to compare you
to golden-haired Helen
is not unseemly.

Now she is conspicuous
among Lydian women as the
rosy-fingered moon at sunset,
surpassing all the stars,
as it spreads light equally
over salt-water sea and flowery
fields, beautiful with dew and
blooming roses, chervil, and
flowering sweet clover.
And often, turning to and fro,
she thinks of gentle Atthis,
and her heart is consumed with longing.

In my mother's time,
if locks were bound in purple,
it was a great adornment;
but she whose long hair
falls fire-yellow red
should wreathe it in blooming flowers.

I loved you, Atthis, once, long ago.
You seemed to me a small, ungraceful girl.

ॐ

You came, and I was
yearning for you;
you cooled my heart,
burning with desire.

ॐ

May you sleep on the breast
of your tender companion.

ॐ

Now, even the thought
of me is hateful
to you, Atthis, and
you fly to Andromeda.

ॐ

Here, now, I shall sing
beautifully, to delight my companions.

Someone, I tell you,
will remember us,
in another time.

❧

Remember that in our youth
we, too, did such things.

❧

Never, I am sure,
will any girl who sees
the light of day approach
you in skill, at any time.

❧

and dappled leather thongs
covered her feet—beautiful
work of Lydia.

❧

and you have forgotten me,
or love another one more.

❧

Toward you, lovely ones,
my thoughts do not change.

when nightlongness overcomes them

ð

and in their eyes,
the black sleep of night

ð

Mnasidica—shapelier than delicate Gyrinno

ð

with what eyes?

ð

O lovely, O graceful one!

ð

and I long and yearn

ð

my pain drips down

ð

you roast us

ð

as long as you wish

ð

WEDDING SONGS (EPITHALAMIA)

Raise up the roof-tree—
a wedding song!
High up, carpenters—
a wedding song!
The bridegroom is coming,
the equal of Ares,
much bigger than a big man.

≥.

To what do I compare you most,
dear bridegroom?
To a slender young shoot
I compare you most.

≥.

Happy bridegroom: the wedding
you prayed for has happened;
the girl you prayed for is yours.

Your form is graceful;
from your eyes, love pours
over your beautiful face.
Aphrodite has favored you greatly.

≥.

For never until now,
bridegroom, was there
another girl like this one.

The doorkeeper's feet
are seven fathoms long;
his sandals are made
of five oxhides,
the hard work of
ten cobblers.

෧

"Virginity, virginity, where have
you gone, leaving me behind?"

"I shall never come back to you,
never come back."

෧

Do I still long for my virginity?

෧

Farewell, bride; farewell, honored bridegroom.

෧

MISCELLANEOUS

I have a child, lovely
as golden flowers,
my darling Cleis,
for whom I would not all Lydia...

But when you die, you will lie there,
and not ever be remembered afterward;
nor will anyone long for you
who have no part in the roses
of Pieria; but unseen instead
you will flit among the shadowy dead.

For Pelagon the fisherman,
his father Meniscus set up
his oar and basket—
remembrances of an unhappy life.

Stars around the lovely moon
hide their brightness, especially
when full she shines over all
the earth.

These are the ashes of Timas,
who died before marriage,
and was received in Persephone's
dark bridal chamber;
and all her companions—
in token of sorrow—
took newly-sharpened iron
and cut their long, lovely hair.

Like the sweet apple that reddens
high on a bough—the highest bough—
which the apple-pickers have
forgotten; not forgotten,
but are not able to reach.

❧

Like a mountain hyacinth
which the herdsmen trample underfoot,
and on the ground the purple...

❧

For he who is beautiful
appears beautiful;
but he who is good
is beautiful therefore.

For those I treat best
hurt me most, and I know it.

≈

But I am not of a spiteful
disposition; I have a gentle heart.

≈

For me, neither honey
nor the honey-bee.

little-voiced

&

soft-voiced

&

sweet-voiced

&

honey-voiced

&

a delicate girl picking flowers

for day is near

&

of all stars, the fairest

&

everywhere glory, shining

&

golden-haired Helen

&

Surpassing, as the Lesbian singer
is to others

messenger of spring,
the lovely-voiced nightingale

⁊

much sweeter than a lyre,
more golden than gold

⁊

Once, they say, Leda found an egg
the color of hyacinth.

⁊

I do not know what to do:
I am of two minds.

⁊

I do not suppose to touch the sky.

⁊

Why me, Irana, daughter of Pandion, the swallow?

The moon has set,
and the Pleiades. In the middle
of the night, time passes by me,
and I lie alone.

ಸ

Glossary

ABANTHIS:

  a pupil or companion of Sappho.

ADONIS:

  mortal loved by Aphrodite. He rejected her in favor of the hunt, and was killed by a boar. His death was lamented annually by Greek girls.

ANACTORIA:

  a pupil or companion of Sappho.

ANDROMEDA:

  a pupil or companion of Sappho.

APHRODITE:

  goddess of love and beauty; also called Cytheria, Cypris, Cyprian, Cyprus-born.

APOLLO:

  sun god; also the god of the lyre, and of poetry and music; son of LETO (see below) and ZEUS (see below).

ARES:

  god of war.

ARTEMIS:

  chaste huntress, sister of APOLLO (see LETO).

ATTHIS:

  a pupil or companion of Sappho.

CLEIS:

  Sappho's only child, named after Sappho's mother.

CRONOS:

  husband of RHEA and father of ZEUS; no longer involved in human affairs.

DICA:

short for MNASIDICA, a pupil or companion of Sappho.

DORICHA:

a famous courtesan, allegedly involved with one of Sappho's brothers.

EROS (CUPID):

servant of APHRODITE, and youngest of the gods.

GONGYLA:

a pupil or companion of Sappho.

GRACES:

attendants of APHRODITE; they bring joy and gratitude into the lives and hearts of humans.

HELEN:

the Helen of Troy.

HERMIONE:

a pupil or companion of Sappho.

LEDA:

mother of HELEN by ZEUS, in the form of a swan.

LETO:

mother, by ZEUS, of APOLLO and ARTEMIS. When the mortal NIOBE boasted that she had borne many more sons and daughters than LETO had, APOLLO and ARTEMIS slew all of them, literally reducing NIOBE to tears, which flowed from a black rock into which she had been transformed. Sappho refers to LETO as the daughter of Coeus.

MUSES:

the nine goddesses of the various arts; sources of inspiration to artists.

NEREIDS:

sea nymphs, daughters of NEREUS; could assist mariners in making safe passage.

NIOBE:

see LETO, above.

PANDION:

father of Procne. Having killed her husband and child in a fit of madness caused by her husband, Procne was saved from death by being changed into a swallow.

PERSEPHONE:

daughter of DEMETER and wife of HADES, hence, queen of the underworld.

PIERIA:

area near Mount Olympos, home of the MUSES (above).

TIMAS:

a pupil or companion of Sappho.

ZEUS:

according to Homer, "the father of gods and men"; hence, the chief deity.

இ

About the Translator

Frank Salvidio was born in Shrewsbury, Massachusetts, and grew up in Norwich, Connecticut. He received a bachelor's degree in philosophy from Columbia University, and also holds M.A.s in education (American International College) and English (University of Connecticut), as well as a Ph.D. in English (University of Connecticut). He is the author of *Between Troy & Florence*, a collection of original poems and translations (Black Swan Books), and a translation of Dante's *Vita Nuova* (Aegina Press). At present, he is living in western Massachusetts, where his daughter Rachel is a student at the College of Our Lady of the Elms.